T0274635

'Not words, letters; not letters, shapes; not shapes, figures; not figures, ciphers; not ciphers, ornaments; not ornaments, decoration; not decoration, semiotics; not semiotics, communicative possibilities; not vagrant potential, slowly forming inflection; not melting deflection, language as dance: in, out, upside down, flapping, flipping, all ways round.'
– Charles Bernstein, recipient 2019 Bollingen Prize for American Poetry

'"When most of the language we consume is non-poetic, should poetry not attempt to poetically intervene within these spaces that are not traditionally poetic?" The answer to Derek Beaulieu's question, put forward in his beautiful essay, is surely yes: the ten brilliantly adventurous visual poems in his *Surface Tension* make a startling case for his fascinating Letraset / photocopier inventions. Beaulieu's compositions originate in a place of clean design and logical narrative; soon, as in a dream, they open up, ushering in what he calls "a poetry of difference, chance, eruption." Marcel Duchamp would have called it the poetry of the infrathin: watch "Simple Symmetry" or "Dendrochronology" open up and come alive in their minutely evolving new spaces. This is quite simply an enchanting book – a book producing new pleasures with each turn of the page.'
– Marjorie Perloff, Sadie Dernham Patek Professor of Humanities, Emerita, Stanford University

'The striking compositions you'll find in *Surface Tension* are being presented sequentially in book form, yet that they wouldn't be out of place hanging on the wall goes without saying. Beaulieu swerves Gomringer when writing that "Readability is the key: like a logo, a poem should be instantly recognizable ... " yet, to this reader, these works merit sustained and enthusiastic viewing precisely because they teeter on the edge of legibility. The kinetic, glitchy quality of their "alphabetic strangeness" keeps them unrecognizable as poems and, here, "that is poetry as I need it," to quote Cage. Think of them as anti-advertisings selling you nothing but bountiful manifestations of the irreducible plasticity of numbers, punctuation marks, and letter forms. No logos.'

– Mónica de la Torre, Madelon Leventhal Rand Endowed Chair in Literature, Brooklyn College; co-editor of *Women in Concrete Poetry 1959–1979*

'With his distinctive visual palindromes and angled axes of symmetry, Derek Beaulieu has developed a signature mastery of Letraset, leveraging the twentieth-century technology as a vehicle for bring concrete poetry into the twenty-first century. With *Surface Tension*, Beaulieu takes the possibilities of that new idiom even further, unsettling the fixity his symmetries once reinforced and dislodging the set in Letraset as poems distort in fun-house-mirror swerves, sag as if under their own weight, pool and smear in the liquid logic of heated ink, or swoop and blur as if in motion. In the process, these poems make visible the filmic potential of the photocopier, the facture of abraded transfers from brittling stock, and the three-dimensional substrate of the page with its flexible bends in curving space. These are thus poems in part about their own modes of production. They are beautiful products of a self-aware and intelligent process.'

– Craig Dworkin, author of *Radium of the Word: A Poetics of Materiality*

SURFACE TENSION

Derek Beaulieu

COACH HOUSE BOOKS, TORONTO

first edition

 Canada Council **Conseil des Arts**
for the Arts   du Canada

Published with the generous assistance of the Canada Council for the Arts and the Ontario
Arts Council. Coach House Books also acknowledges the support of the Government of
Canada through the Canada Book Fund and the Government of Ontario through the Ontario
Book Publishing Tax Credit.

LIBRARY AND ARCHIVES CANADA CATALOGUING IN PUBLICATION

Title: Surface tension / Derek Beaulieu.
Names: Beaulieu, D. A. (Derek Alexander), author.
Description: Poems.
Identifiers: Canadiana (print) 20220190593 | Canadiana (ebook) 20220190615 | ISBN
9781552454503 (softcover) | ISBN 9781770567412 (EPUB) | ISBN 9781770567429 (PDF)
Classification: LCC PS8553.E223 S87 2022 | DDC C811/.54—dc23

Surface Tension is available as an ebook: ISBN 978 1 77056 741 2 (EPUB)

Purchase of the print version of this book entitles you to a free digital copy. To claim your
ebook of this title, please email sales@chbooks.com with proof of purchase. (Coach House
Books reserves the right to terminate the free digital download offer at any time.)

TABLE OF CONTENTS

KURSIV

For Jenni B. Baker, in memoriam

PERFORMANCE ADJUSTMENT/APPEAL PROCESS

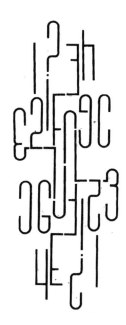

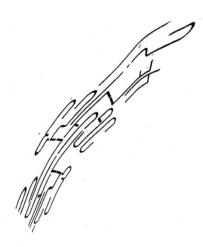

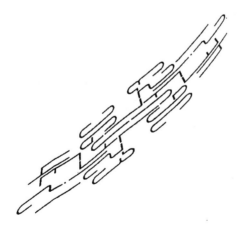

MADGE, YOU'RE SOAKING IN IT

At its core, *Surface Tension* holds a series of delicate, balanced poems, each symmetrical, palindromic, and made by hand using Letraset. A graphic designer's tool, Letraset – which standardized typefaces across advertising platforms in an idealistic, 1950s/60s aesthetic of sales copy and purchasing power – foregrounds a clean design; a logical, controllable narrative of graphic beauty and heroic lyricism.

Much contemporary poetry arose from that mandate, but we can swerve the beauty away from the sales pitch.

Surface Tension creates landscapes from the remnants of advertising (Letraset, for instance, is now mostly used by scrapbookers and hobbyists), a pastoral space of deep ink-pools where even the language itself is an oily sheen on the surface of writing.

Just as logos continuously wash over us, let poetry do the same; part of the written landscape we occupy.

These reflections and distortions work to keep concrete current, in flow, a fluidity refusing to solidify around power.

The most representative (and perhaps even the most exciting) art form of our age is the advertising logo. Why not create a logo advertising modern poetry, modern art?

Poetry moves toward formal simplification, abbreviated statements on all levels of communication from the headline and the advertising slogan to the scientific formula – the quick, concentrated visual message, in other words.

Remarkable words with letters bigger than aqueducts ringed with quick-silver, flamboyant and shocking, like advertising.

EUPHEMIA ASLEEP

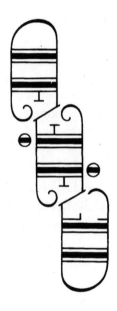

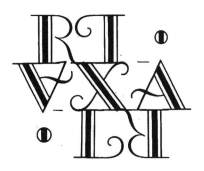

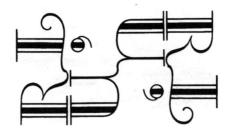

FORM IS NEVER MORE THAN AN EXTENSION OF CONTENT

The poems are further manipulated using photocopiers to become liquid and languid, troubling poetic logic, perfection, and power narratives, they flow and gather, drip and congeal, sliding off the page.

Photocopiers don't just reproduce invoices and documents, they introduce beauty and sway, noise and reverb.

Literature is not craftsmanship but an industrial process where the poem is a prototype rather than artistry.

The contemporary poem is an understanding of juxtaposition. It focuses on the arrangement of letters and material. Headlines, slogans, groups of sounds and letters give rise to forms that could be models for a new poetry just waiting to be taken up for use.

That use has now arrived.

If the poem is a new product in a world flooded with new products, then it must partake of the nature of the world that created it.

When most of the language we consume is non-poetic, should poetry not attempt to poetically intervene within these spaces that are not traditionally poetic?

Poetry is not the beautiful expression of emotive truths; it is the archaeological rearrangement of the remains of an ancient civilization.

Poetry can fully embrace the plasticized space of graphics and glyphs, pixels and projections.

Embody the immediate present, the place where poetry is using the language of contemporary existence.

Write not just in the margins, but in the kerning.

Reading has shifted from something that takes place over time (an investment occurring privately; i.e., single readers quietly reading single books) to something that takes place instantaneously (a moment occurring publicly; i.e., momentary scans of logos, headlines, and brand recognition).

Imagine a poetry that learns from the internet, learns from mass media, and starts to assume different forms of distribution: the website, the tweet, the post, the logo, the advertisement, the targeted ad.

Poets don't own their work; they just borrow it from the dictionary.

SIMPLE SYMMETRY

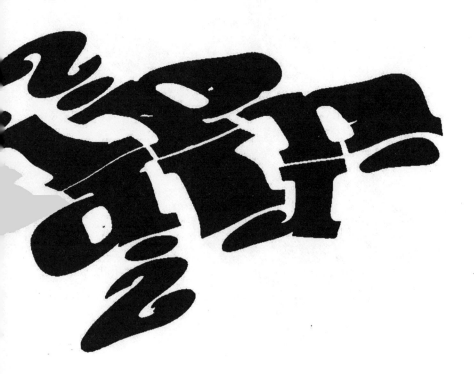

AMPERSANDANCE
For Gary Barwin

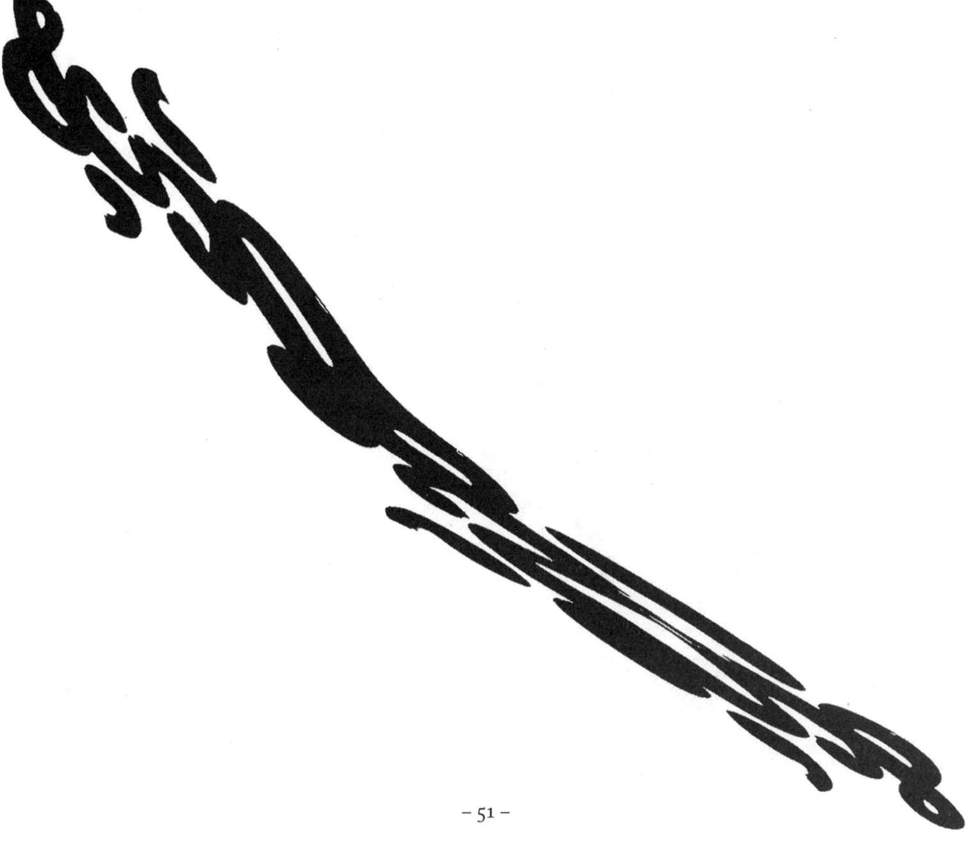

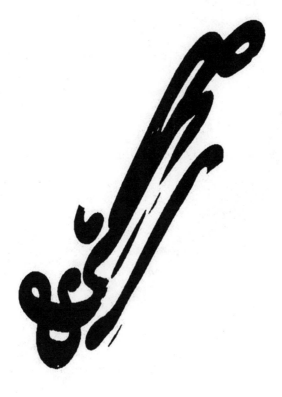

ALL THAT SIGNIFIES CAN BE SOLD

Poetry, like advertising, is anything you can get away with.

Readability is key: like a logo, a poem should be instantly recognizable. Poetry, here, endeavours to render all language into poetic icons, much like how everyone can understand the meaning of a folder icon on the computer screen.

The contemporary poem as a form most closely echoes the icons used in contemporary computing – the file-folder icon, the floppy disk save icon – not to mention the cool typography of the Mac platform and icon-driven iPad.

While graphic design, advertising, and contemporary design culture expand to redefine and rewrite how we understand communication, poetry struggles against becoming ensconced in the traditional.

The McDonald's golden arches, the Nike swoosh, and the Apple logo best represent the aims of contemporary poets.

No one can possibly recognize their mother tongue when printed in Futura typeface. It lacks maternal warmth, it lacks friendliness.

Like logos for the corporate sponsors of Jorge Luis Borges's Library of Babel, these poems use the particles of language to represent and promote goods and corporations just out of reach.

These imaginary businesses, and the advertising campaigns that support them, promote a poetic dreamscape of alphabetic strangeness.

Poems are the street signs, the signage, the advertising logos for the shops and corporations that are just beyond reach.

How far away from poetry can we get and still be writing and reading poetry?

Moments of poetic nostalgia for the signposts of a non-existent past.

Make it simple. Make it memorable. Make it inviting to look at.

A poetry of difference, chance, and eruption.

You complain that this stuff is not written in English. It is not written at all. It is not to be read – or rather it is not only to be read. It is to be looked at and listened to.

Language to be looked at and/or things to be read.

CIRCUIT

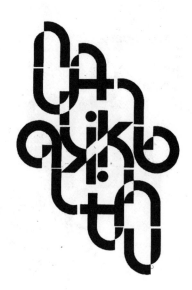

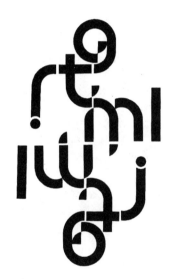

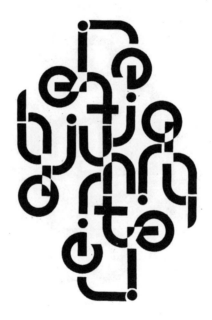

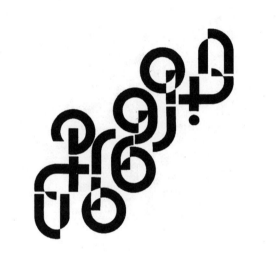

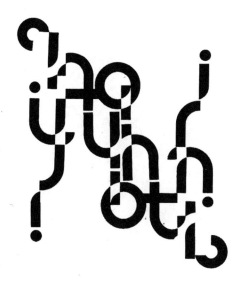

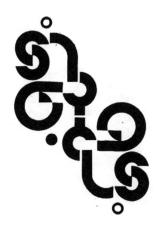

FAFNIR

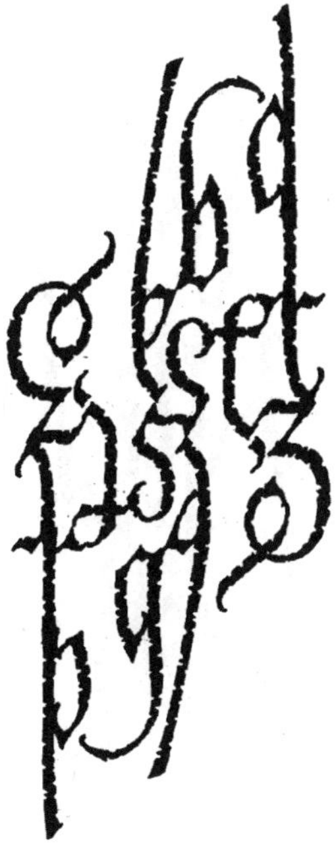

TYPE IS WHAT MEANING LOOKS LIKE

The logic of the symmetries is a closed case of beauty, and these distortions present not just a puddle but an ocean, a flowing openness of poetic possibility where the format and authority of letters and clockwork slide away to present a more liquid, a more natural, a more warm and welcoming unmoored form of poetic.

They aren't stains; they're pools. There's space here, active surfaces, ponds with depth.

Poems are not rarefied jewels carefully chiselled for a bespoke audience, they are nuts and bolts, factory made, shifting from use to use; they are airport signs manufactured in bulk, they are silkscreens awaiting T-shirts.

Poetry can move past declarations of emotion into a form more indicative of how readers process language.

It is the realization that the usages of language in poetry of the traditional type are not keeping pace with live processes of language and rapid methods of communication at work in the contemporary world.

Writing is not *about* something; it is that something itself.

It is precisely this distancing from traditional poetics that makes visual poetry both a marginalized form unrecognizable to many poets and a genre perfectly suited to a twenty-first-century readership.

Poetry here is concerned with being an object to be perceived rather than read; the content of the poem is non-literary but completely recognizable.

These poems begin in recognition: as soon as we see them, we know a particular object is in question because only that object has just this (and no other) emblem.

CIRCUITBREAKER

PAGE BREAK

For Bob Cobbing, Jennifer Pike Cobbing, and Lawrence Upton, in memoriam

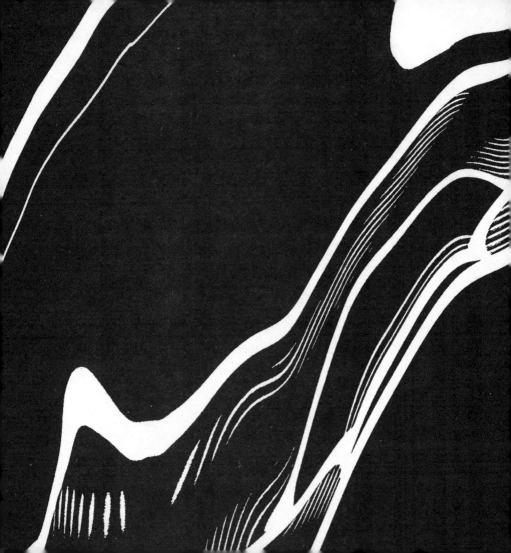

A POEM SHOULD NOT MEAN

The poem is the result of a concentration upon the physical material upon which the poem or text is made.

Emotions and ideas are not physical materials.

Poems that refold the old, retrieved from a nowhere cultural memory, fitfully nostalgic for an ethereal, ephemeral moment.

Poems made of letters that combine, like so many pieces of orphaned Lego, to form previously unexpected constructions not at all resembling the images on the packaging.

Poets owe nothing to 'poetry,' least of all deference.

Every page should explode because of its staggering absurdity, the enthusiasm of its principles, or its typography.

Poetry belongs to the world of appearances, not to that of actual use.

Poems that refuse linearity in favour of the momentary.

A poem should not mean /

but be.

DENDROCHRONOLOGY

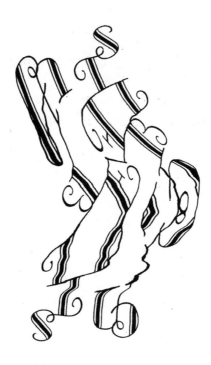

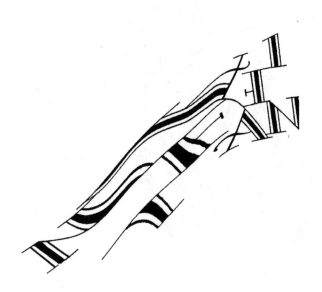

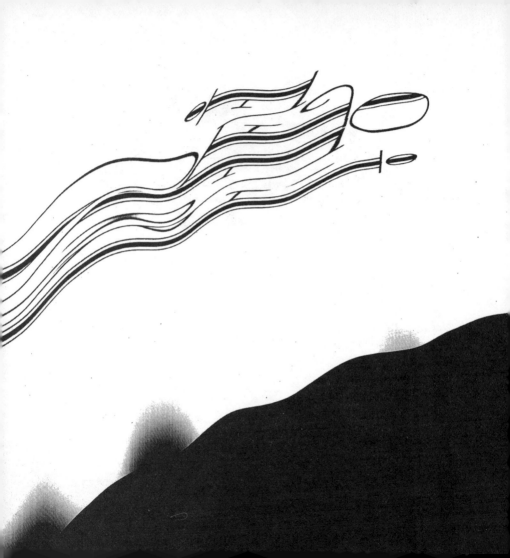

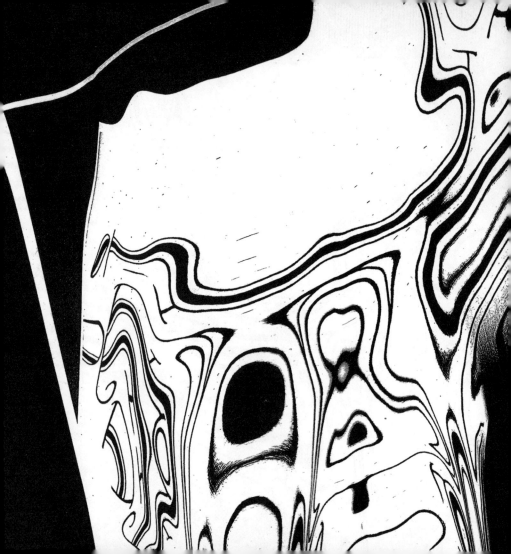

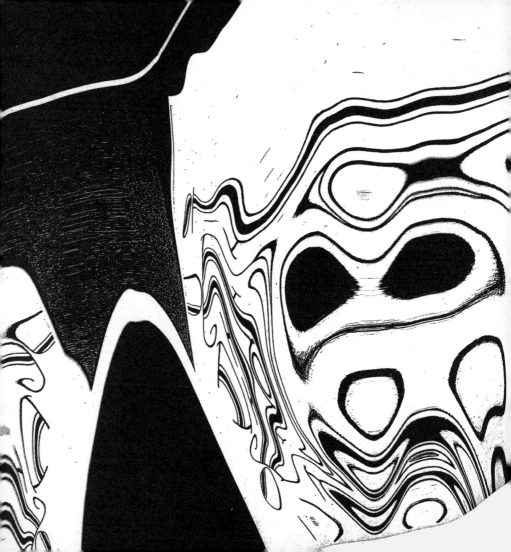

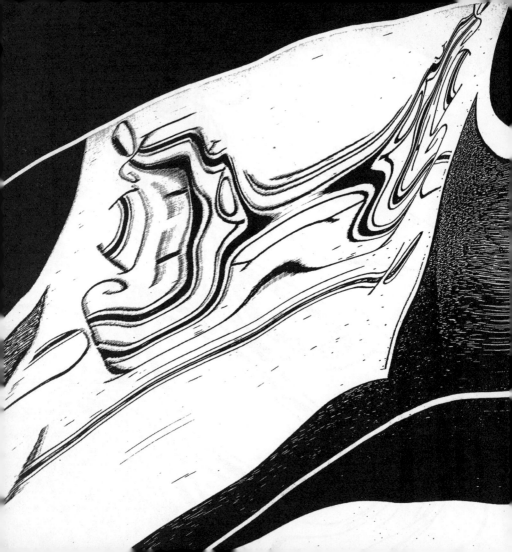

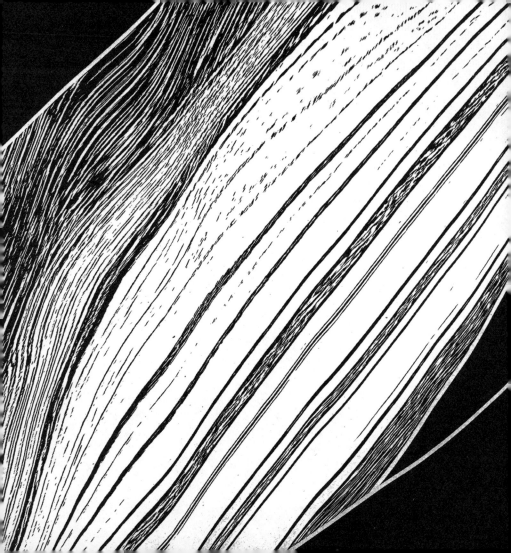

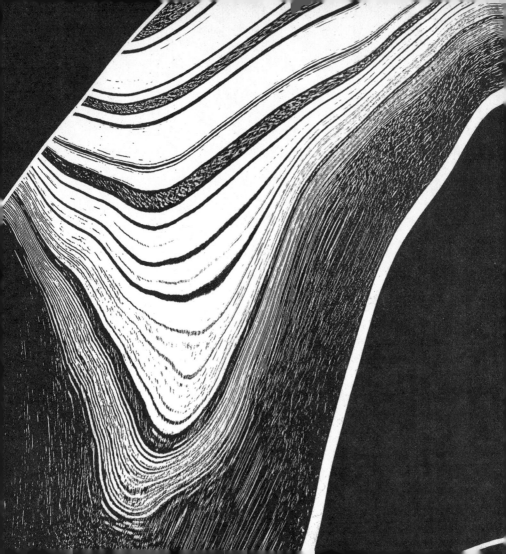

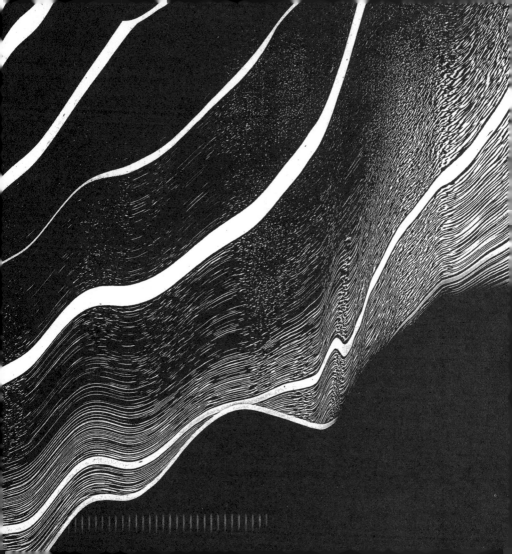

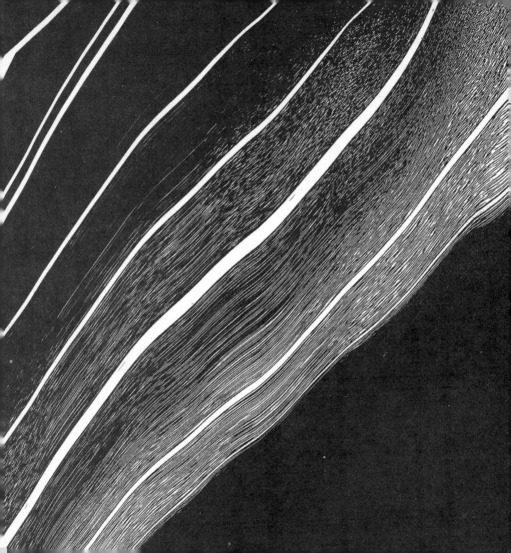

ACKNOWLEDGEMENTS

Surface Tension is dedicated to the memory of Jenni B. Baker, Bob Cobbing, Jennifer Pike Cobbing, and Lawrence Upton.

Excerpts from *Surface Tension* have appeared in small press editions and anthologies from *Container*, *Paper View Books*, *Penteract*, *Poems for All*, *Puddles of Sky*, *No Press*, *Whiskeyjack*, and in *A minor*, *Anamorphoseis*, *The Capilano Review*, *Love Love*, *Periodicities*, *Pocket Lint*, and *ToCall* magazines – thank you to the editors and publishers for helping feed and water these poems.

The essay contains comments, many slightly swerved, about poetry and advertising, gathered from across the Greek Chorus of the internet.

Thanks to Gary Barwin, Charles Bernstein, Gregory Betts, Christian Bök, Mónica de la Torre, Kit Dobson, Craig Dworkin, Rhys Farrell, Kenneth Goldsmith, Helen Hajnoczky, Peter Jaeger, Kaley Kramer, Simon Morris, Sal Nunchakov, Astra Papachristodoulou, Marjorie Perloff, and Jordan Scott for their friendship, conversation, inspiration, and camaraderie. Everyone at Coach House Books, especially Nasser Hussain, Crystal Sikma, and Alana Wilcox, has provided an incredibly supportive conversation on how poetry can be; thank you.

Thank you, lastly, to Kristen and Maddie for keeping my eyes focused on the right things.

ABOUT THE AUTHOR

Derek Beaulieu is the author/editor of twenty-five collections of poetry, prose, and criticism, including *a, A Novel*, published by France's Jean Boîte Editions, and *Lens Flare*, co-written with Rhys Farrell, published by the UK's Guillemot Press. Beaulieu was Calgary's 2014–16 Poet Laureate and is Banff's 2022–24 Poet Laureate. He has received multiple local and national awards for his teaching and dedication to students and community. Beaulieu has edited volumes of historically important avant-garde work by bill bissett, bpNichol, and John Riddell, several anthologies of new experimental writing, and is the Visual Poetry editor at UbuWeb.

Derek Beaulieu holds a PhD in Creative Writing from Roehampton University and is the Director of Literary Arts at Banff Centre for Arts and Creativity.

He can be found online at www.derekbeaulieu.ca.

BY THE SAME AUTHOR

Poetry

Lens Flare. Co-written with Rhys Farrell, 2021.

Aperture. 2019.

Counter / Weight. 2018.

Ascender / Descender. 2016.

Kern. 2014.

Please, No More Poetry: The Poetry of derek beaulieu. Edited by Kit Dobson, with an afterword by Lori Emerson, 2013.

Kern. 2011.

Silence. 2010.

chains. 2008.

fractal economies. 2006.

frogments from the frag pool: haiku after bashō. Co-written with Gary Barwin, 2005.

with wax. 2003.

Prose

a, A Novel. With an afterword by Gilda Williams, 2017.

Konzeptuelle Arbeiten. 2017.

The Unbearable Contact with Poets. 2015.

Local Colour: Ghosts, Variations. Edited by Ola Ståhl, 2012.

Seen of the Crime: Essays on Conceptual Writing. 2011.

How to Write. 2010.

Local Colour. 2008.

Flatland: a romance of many dimensions. With an afterword by Marjorie Perloff, 2006.

Edited Collections

bpNichol. *Nights on Prose Mountain: The Fiction of bpNichol,* 2018.

The Calgary Renaissance. Co-edited with rob mclennan, 2016.

John Riddell. *Writing Surfaces: Selected Fiction of John Riddell.* Co-edited with Lori Emerson, 2013.

bill bissett. *RUSH: what fuckan theory; a study uv language.* Co-edited with Gregory Betts, 2012.

Shift and Switch: New Canadian Poetry. Co-edited with Jason Christie and angela rawlings, 2005.

Typeset in Goluska and Futura.

Printed at the Coach House on bpNichol Lane in Toronto, Ontario, on Rolland paper. This book was printed with vegetable-based ink on a 1973 Heidelberg KORD offset litho press. Its pages were folded on a Baumfolder, gathered by hand, bound on a Sulby Auto-Minabinda, and trimmed on a Polar single-knife cutter.

Coach House is on the traditional territory of many nations, including the Mississaugas of the Credit, the Anishnabeg, the Chippewa, the Haudenosaunee, and the Wendat peoples, and is now home to many diverse First Nations, Inuit, and Métis peoples. We acknowledge that Toronto is covered by Treaty 13 with the Mississaugas of the Credit. We are grateful to live and work on this land.

Edited for the press by Nasser Hussain
Cover and interior design by Crystal Sikma
Author photo by Ricky Adam

Coach House Books
80 bpNichol Lane
Toronto ON M5S 3J4
Canada

416 979 2217
800 367 6360
mail@chbooks.com
www.chbooks.com

PRINTED IN CANADA ON CANADIAN PAPER
by mindless acid freaKs